SUPERCHARGED SPORTS

HIGH-TECH SPORTS SCIENCE

PAULA JOHANSON

CRABTREE
Publishing Company
www.crabtreebooks.com

Author: Paula Johanson

Editors: Sarah Eason, John Andrews, and Petrice Custance

Proofreader and indexer: Wendy Scavuzzo

Editorial director: Kathy Middleton

Design: Paul Myerscough, Paul Oakley, and Jane McKenna

Cover design: Paul Myerscough

Photo research: Rachel Blount

Production coordinator and Prepress technician: Margaret Amy Salter

Print coordinator: Margaret Amy Salter

Consultant: David Hawksett

Produced for Crabtree Publishing Company by Calcium Creative.

Photo Credits:

t=Top, tr=Top Right, tl=Top Left, b=Bottom, br=Bottom Right, bl=Bottom Left, bc=Bottom Center, r=Right

Catapult Sports: 19; Cervélo Cycles Inc.: 1, 11; Force Impact Technologies Inc.: 23b; Roborace: 26–27; Shutterstock: Mitrofanov Alexander 5b, Aaron Amat 28t, Fabio Balbi 25, Paolo Bona 6, Brocreative 5tl, Capture Light 14, Diego Cervo 20–21, Devrimerdogan 15, Lauren Elisabeth 24, Four Oaks 29bc, Halfpoint 22–23, Mehaniq 16, Ms.nen 22r, Ostill 17, Slavoljub Pantelic 9t, 29br, Jamie Roach 4, Oskar SCHULER 29tr, Sianstock 6–7, Jeff Smith – Perspectives 27t, Sportpoint 12–13, Stock-Asso 3, 12b, StudioOneNine 5tr, Lilyana Vynogradova 8–9, Sander van der Werf 18; Wikimedia Commons: Bibliothèque nationale de France 28br, Horge 29tl, Jen_ross83 10, Eadweard Muybridge/Library of Congress 28bl.

Cover: Cambridge Consultants (foreground); Shutterstock: Aspen Photo (bkgd);

Library and Archives Canada Cataloguing in Publication

Johanson, Paula, 1961-, author
Supercharged sports / Paula Johanson.

(Techno planet)
Includes index.
Issued in print and electronic formats.
ISBN 978-0-7787-3603-5 (hardcover).--
ISBN 978-0-7787-3617-2 (softcover).--
ISBN 978-1-4271-1991-9 (HTML)

1. Sports--Technological innovations--Juvenile literature. 2. Sports sciences--Juvenile literature. 3. Sporting goods--Juvenile literature. I. Title.

GV745.J64 2017 j688.7′6 C2017-903595-9 C2017-903596-7

Library of Congress Cataloging-in-Publication Data

Names: Johanson, Paula, author.
Title: Supercharged sports / Paula Johanson.
Description: New York, NY : Crabtree Publishing Company, [2018] | Series: Techno planet | Includes index. | Audience: Age 8-11. | Audience: Grade 7 to 8.
Identifiers: LCCN 2017027477 (print) | LCCN 2017031794 (ebook) | ISBN 9781427119919 (Electronic HTML) | ISBN 9780778736035 (reinforced library binding : alk. paper) | ISBN 9780778736172 (pbk. : alk. paper)
Subjects: LCSH: Sports--Technological innovations--Juvenile literature.
Classification: LCC GV745 (ebook) | LCC GV745 .J64 2018 (print) | DDC 688.7/6--dc23
LC record available at https://lccn.loc.gov/2017027477

Crabtree Publishing Company
www.crabtreebooks.com 1-800-387-7650

Printed in Canada/092017/PB20170719

Published in Canada
Crabtree Publishing
616 Welland Ave.
St. Catharines, Ontario
L2M 5V6

Published in the United States
Crabtree Publishing
PMB 59051
350 Fifth Avenue, 59th Floor
New York, New York 10118

Published in the United Kingdom
Crabtree Publishing
Maritime House
Basin Road North, Hove
BN41 1WR

Published in Australia
Crabtree Publishing
3 Charles Street
Coburg North
VIC, 3058

CONTENTS

SPORTS TECH

All sports use technology. Technology is the use of science to invent new things or make things work better. Athletes and coaches use technology to improve performance. Officials such as referees use technology to ensure fair play. Fans use technology, too, to watch broadcasts, calculate statistics, and more. Even those who play sports just for fun benefit from technology. Sometimes, technology is the most fun part of sports!

SOME THINGS DO NOT CHANGE

Technology has been used in sports throughout history. In Ancient Greece, a starting gate called a hysplex was developed for races. It ensured all runners got a fair start. A rope barrier, stretching in front of the racers, was connected to a post at each end of the starting line. At the start, the posts were released, which made the rope barrier fall, and all the runners could begin the race. Versions of the hysplex are still used today.

Carvings on Ancient Egyptian monuments show a game being played with a ball. The best technical skills of that time went into making the balls. They were made of leather coverings that were stuffed with plants or hay, then stitched together by hand. Today, soccer balls are still made in a similar way, with the leather coverings still often stitched by hand, but the balls are now filled with air.

*Racing wheelchairs use light metal **alloys** like those used in aircraft and space probes.*

BETTER WITH TECH

Modern technology has made major advances in the quality and function of sports equipment.

For example, the new miCoach Smart Ball is designed to help people improve their soccer skills. A **sensor** in the middle of the ball tracks the speed, height, and direction of the ball when the ball is kicked. The **data** is sent to a smartphone, which tracks the user's progress.

Technology is providing ways to improve player performance while also improving player safety, such as with stronger helmets and health-monitoring devices. Technology has also helped make sports more inclusive. Athletes with disabilities are now being provided with better tools, such as high-tech wheelchairs, which allow them to take part in sports at the highest levels. These are exciting times in the world of sports!

Old sports helmets were a move in the right direction. New helmets are stronger, lighter, and more effective.

Hockey was one of the first sports to use video technology to help officials make decisions.

NEW CAMERA ANGLES

Leland Stanford, the founder of Stanford University in California, was a fan of horse racing. In 1872, he hired a photographer to prove that a running horse lifts all four feet off the ground at once. Ever since, cameras have been used in many different ways in sports. They decide scores, settle bets, and record every move. New technology has opened up new ways for people to see a game, whether they are athletes, officials, or spectators.

CAUGHT ON FILM

Coaches and athletes in sports such as baseball, basketball, and golf use video **analysis**. They film themselves in action, then look at the video to see how they can play better. Referees and officials use cameras for **playback**. They do this to make sure their decisions are correct and fair. They do not want to miss out on counting a goal or spotting a **penalty**.

At international soccer matches, drone cameras can record action from all the right angles.

Many cameras are still held by hand. However, cameras can also be attached to high posts or cables above the playing field and operated by computer. The latest drone technology means the camera can move almost anywhere. With these added viewpoints, television broadcasts are more interesting to watch. Good camera work improves audience enjoyment. It can make people watching *Hockey Night in Canada* feel as though they are actually in the arena!

*Headcams are no longer very costly. They are now commonly used by both **amateur** and professional athletes.*

TECHNO PLANET

Drones with cameras can capture new angles at sports events. Quadcopter drones, with four rotary blades, are the most stable for camera work. With video taken from overhead, games and practices are easier for coaches and players to analyze. Video recordings can be fed into analysis software, such as Sportscode, which can then be studied by players and coaches.

CAMERAS FOR EVERYONE

Now even amateur athletes use cameras. They can wear GoPro headcams to take videos of what they are doing to watch later for fun and to share with friends or the public. They can also analyze the video to see how they can improve their performance. It is handy technology —and you do not have to be a rocket scientist to use it!

SIGNALING TECH

Sports officials use technology to help them make the right decisions. Professional hockey used goal-line cameras and sensors to tell officials whether a puck has crossed a goal line. The cameras make for exciting television, too! Professional soccer has started using goal-line cameras, as well.

MAKING A HIT

In fencing competitions, fencers wear jackets with metallic fibers. Their swords and jackets are plugged into an **electronic circuit**, and players compete on a long strip of woven metal threads. Even the lightest of touches cause the circuit to signal a hit has been made.

EYES LIKE A HAWK

Ever lose sight of a moving ball? Tennis competitions use technology to track ball movement. It helps tennis umpires decide if a ball lands in or out of the court. This technology is called Hawk-Eye. Up to 10 cameras track the exact movement of the tennis ball, which is then turned into a video picture by **virtual reality** computer software. It makes the game fairer and is exciting to watch.

Hawk-Eye was launched in England in 2001. It is now used in more than 20 sports. The technology first appeared in cricket, the second most popular sport in the world. It gave the television viewer more information on the movement of the cricket ball. Umpires can also use technologies called Hot Spot and UltraEdge. Hot Spot uses **infrared** cameras to show whether the ball has touched a batter's bat. UltraEdge uses cameras and microphones to pick up even the slightest touch on a bat.

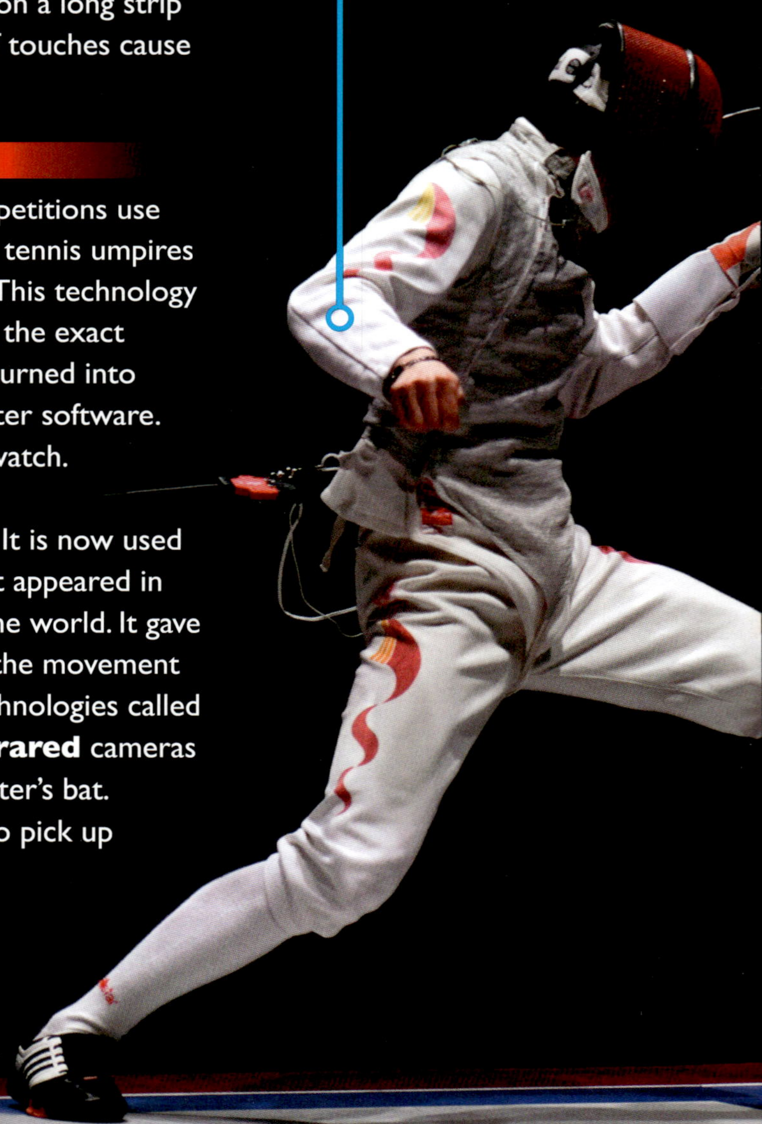

Fast moves in fencing matches are too quick for the eye to follow. Now, electronic circuits record any hits.

WE ARE ALL EXPERTS NOW

Video review systems are becoming smarter every day. They help make decisions in many sports. With comparisons and instant replays, television allows spectators to analyze tactics and statistics in sports as varied as judo, fencing, snooker, badminton, handball, and volleyball. Even a simple game such as soccer can now be examined in exact detail by both professional experts and fans watching at home.

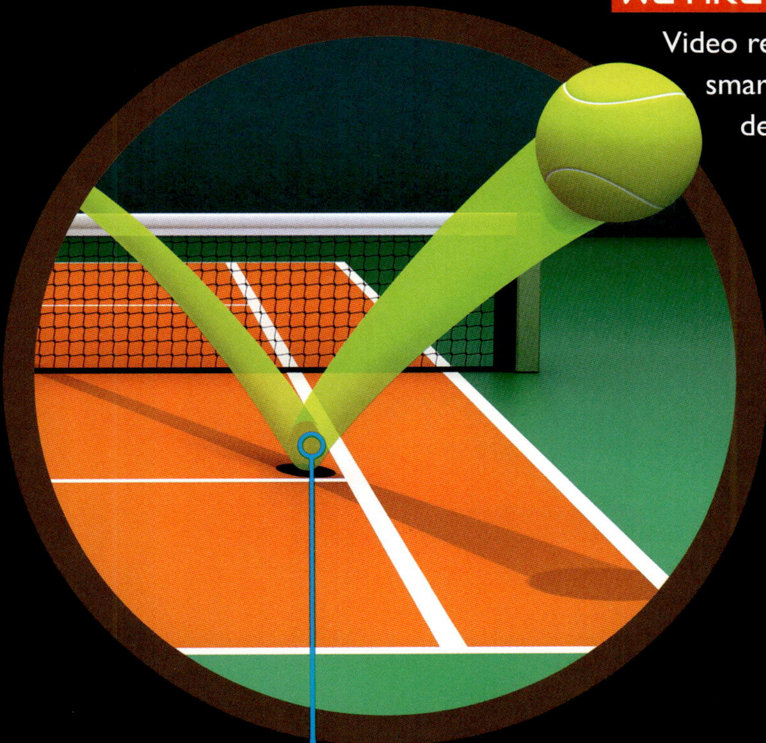

Was that in or out? Hawk-Eye systems keep track of tennis balls in flight.

EQUIPMENT MOVES ON

You cannot play soccer, baseball, or basketball without a ball. You cannot play tennis, badminton, or baseball without a racket or bat. Most sports still use the same basic equipment they have always used. However, new materials and smart designs mean sports can be played better and more safely than ever.

STRONGER AND SAFER

Sensors can be attached to the handle or strings of a tennis racket. These measure data such as speed, shots, and energy. The data is sent wirelessly to a smartphone, where it can be analyzed. The Babolat Play tennis racket has a sensor that is actually built into the handle.

Instead of being carved from wood, equipment from rackets to kayak paddles can be made much lighter and stronger using carbon fibers and **graphene**. Players who use graphene equipment do not tire as quickly, due to the lighter weight. Helmets are now more than a hard leather or plastic shell. Bicycle helmets are shaped for **aerodynamics** and to vent hot air. Batters in baseball and cricket wear helmets padded with shock foam to protect against **concussion**. Football quarterbacks wear radio headsets in their helmets to communicate with coaches.

Race cars are far safer than they used to be. However, drivers are still injured and even killed. New technology is introduced all the time to reduce the risk of accidents. In Formula 1, two new canopy systems, called the "halo" and the "aeroscreen," are being tested. They are fitted to the front of a car's cockpit to protect the driver from flying objects.

Formula 1 drivers can be protected from serious injury by the "halo" canopy system.

GOING FOR SPEED

Racing bicycles can go faster with frames made of carbon fibers or other lightweight metals, such as alloys of aluminum and titanium. Racing bicycles use other technology as well to improve their aerodynamics. Rather than dozens of spokes, their wheels may just have three big spokes, or no spokes at all. A solid, lightweight plastic wheel means less air resistance. In 2016, a Canadian company called Cervélo made the T5GB bicycle for the Great Britain track cycling team. This was probably the world's most aerodynamic bicycle. It helped the team win 12 medals at the Rio Olympics.

Aerodynamic helmets, wheels, and even clothing help track cyclists reach ever-higher speeds.

SPIRIT IN MOTION

Technology allows people with disabilities to take part in many sports, including archery and tennis. Wheelchairs, prosthetics, and other equipment are being designed to help people with disabilities compete at a very high level. This is celebrated most notably every four years in the Paralympic Games that takes place after the Olympics. The motto for the Paralympic Games is "Spirit in Motion."

WHEEL POWER

How do you play a sport when you cannot use your legs? Even people who are **paralyzed** can enjoy sports thanks to wheelchair technology. Wheelchairs for sports such as basketball and rugby are built low and light so players can move and change direction quickly. The wheels are angled so the chair does not tip over. Racing wheelchairs are built for speed, inspired by fighter-jet and race-car technology.

This carbon fiber prosthetic does the work of a lower leg very well, without needing to look like a real leg.

BLADE RUNNERS

Athletes who use artificial legs for sports can run on springy blades made from 80 layers of carbon fiber. Each layer is thinner than a human hair. The blades can be attached to a high-tech "sports knee." This allows more and more people who have lost a limb to take part in running events.

Parts for prosthetics and even whole artificial limbs can now be made using **three-dimensional (3-D)** printers. These printers build up thin layers of plastic into a solid object, based on

Programming for 3-D printers can be learned at public libraries, schools, and colleges.

TECHNO PLANET

If you cannot see, playing sports is very difficult. However, new technology is making it possible for people who are blind to take part. Athletes can wear headsets so a person can warn them of obstacles when racing. The BONX Grip is a powerful wireless earpiece for athletes who are blind, which allows them to keep in touch with a guide, even in noisy outdoor conditions.

a computer image. The cost of an artificial arm or leg can be thousands of dollars. Buying one is expensive. Buying a second prosthetic just for sports is not always possible. Limbs made by a 3-D printer may become an affordable option.

TOO MUCH TECHNOLOGY?

Some athletes with disabilities take part in international sports alongside people with no disabilities. Oscar Pistorius from South Africa ran in the 2012 London Olympics on artificial legs. Did this give him an advantage over other athletes? At what point does technology give people with disabilities an unfair advantage? For now, Olympic officials have said that springy blades have no advantage over working body joints.

DESIGNED BY COMPUTER

In many sports, computer software improves athlete performance and safety. Some improvements are for complex technologies such as cars, motorcycles, and boats. However, it is amazing how changes made to fairly simple tools, such as rugby balls or snowshoes, can improve scores or reduce injuries. Safety is a big priority, but athletes also want to be faster and better!

TECH TWEAKS

A golf ball travels straighter and farther if you hit it on a golf club's "sweet spot." Titanium golf clubs designed with a larger "sweet spot" add yards to a drive with no extra effort. Bobsleds can be made faster and safer by using 3-D design programs to make small but important design adjustments. Canoes and kayaks, as well as the hulls and sails of racing yachts, are being designed to use lighter and stronger materials. Virtual models can be tested and modified on the computer screen before anything is built. Entire ski resorts, golf courses, or stadiums can be planned on computers.

The aerodynamic performance of a Formula 1 car is as important as the person who drives it. Racing teams use the latest technology to test their cars. In the past, tests were done using specially built wind tunnels. Now they use a digital wind tunnel linked to a "supercomputer" as powerful as 90,000 iPhones.

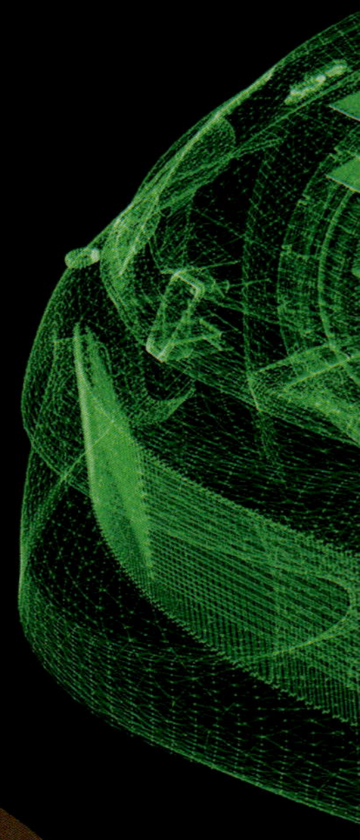

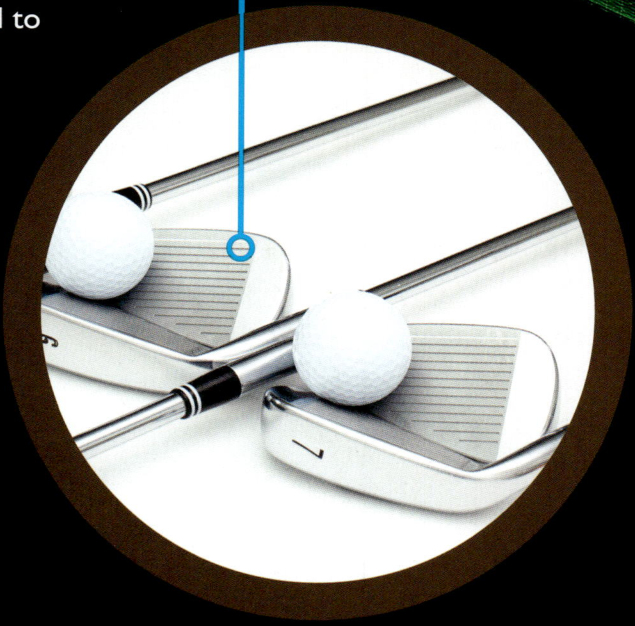

Golf clubs made of titanium are not only light and strong, they also do not rust.

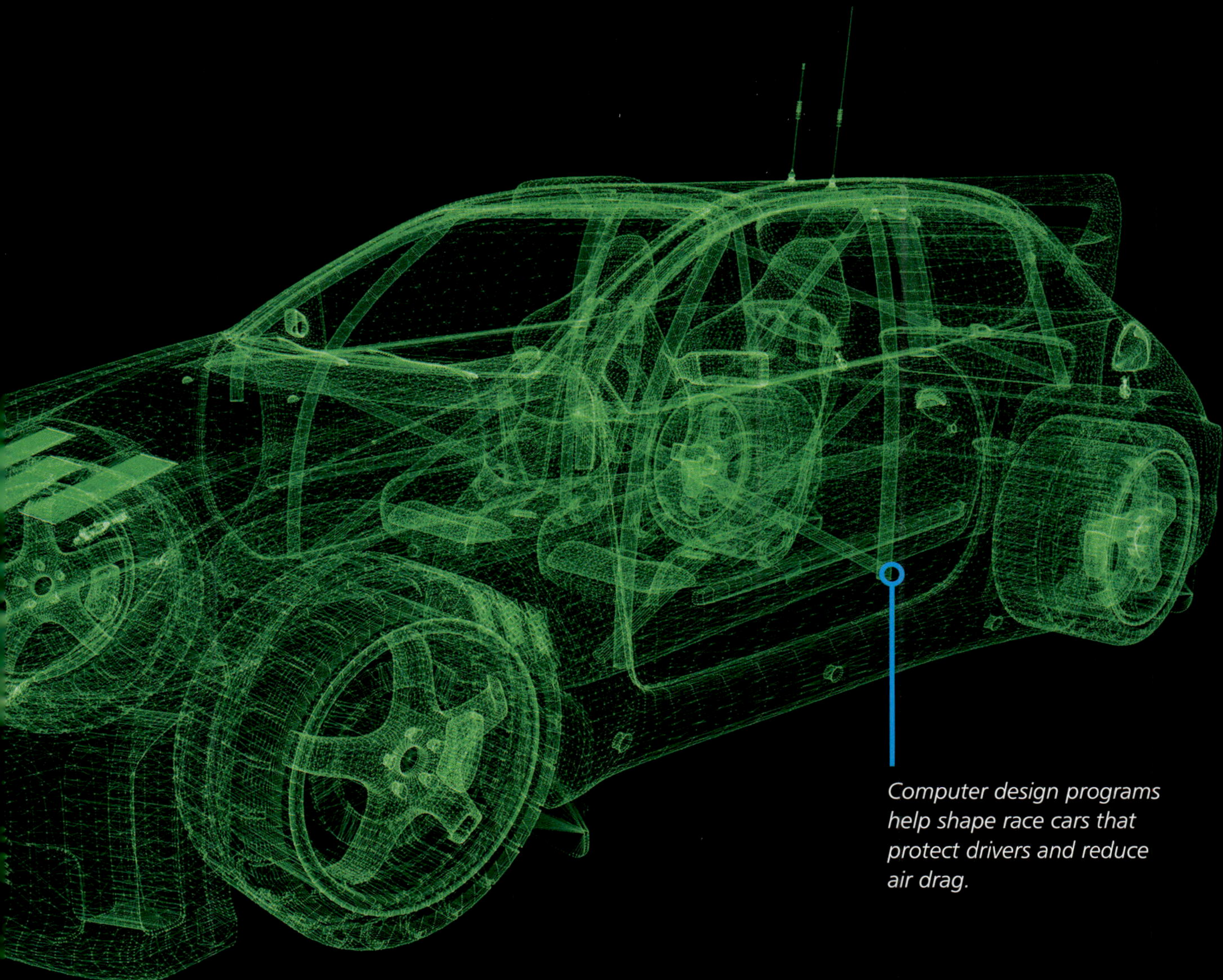

Computer design programs help shape race cars that protect drivers and reduce air drag.

OUT OF REACH?

All this tech and computer knowledge does not come for free. Unless athletes have a **sponsor,** the expense can put the cost of new equipment or personalized training out of reach. Hard work and dedication are not enough to bring an athlete success in international competitions.

In many sports, you will not be successful unless you use the latest technology. How fair is it when some people—and some countries—cannot afford the newest equipment and computer programs? The push to improve a sport can bring an unfair advantage to players who have money or sponsors.

SMART MATERIALS

Whatever the sport, there is a way to dress for it. Sports uniforms have changed little over the years. However, in most sports, new technology is finding new ways of making small gains from what athletes wear. High-tech materials make running shoes and soccer cleats light, but tough. They give hockey and football players stronger padding. Smart materials can improve performance and provide better protection.

WET AND SWEAT

Ever find that your sports clothes have a permanent stink? Body odors do not build up on high-tech shirts. They have silver **ions** in the fibers to reduce biological smells by killing the bacteria that produce them. Tops made from incredibly thin synthetic fibers called **microfibers** wick away sweat to keep the wearer cool and dry. For a more natural alternative, wool from Merino sheep is spun into lightweight fabric for odor-free clothing that is comfortable at every temperature.

Weather is an important factor for enjoying outdoor sports. In rain and snow, people need clothing that keeps them warm and dry. Clothing made of Gore-Tex fabric uses different layers of high-tech materials. This protects a person from the wind and rain, but also allows sweat to pass through.

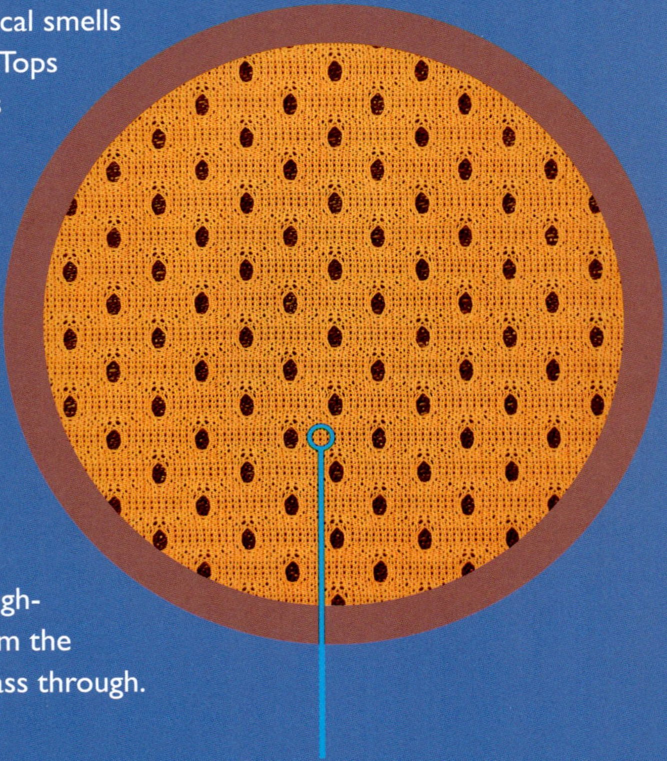

High-tech fabrics with special vents can wick away sweat and keep athletes cool.

BUILT-IN TECH

Some smart materials contain extra technology. The shock-absorber materials made by the D30 company are light and flexible, but very strong on **impact**. They are used inside football, baseball, and hockey helmets. Speedo LZR racer suits for swimmers **compress** the body to make it move through the water more easily. Special supports hold the swimmer higher in the water. Some sportswear fabrics even have sensors to send information to a computer about a person's pulse, temperature, or movements for later analysis.

Triathletes in suits like these can shave seconds off their time in the swimming part of their races.

TECHNO PLANET

New sports need new clothing. An extreme sport, in particular, needs high-tech materials. Wingsuiting is one of the most dangerous sports in the world. It is the sport of flying through the air wearing a suit that works like a bird's wings. The suit is made of very strong, yet very light, fabric. The fabric is also temperature-proof and totally waterproof.

MEASURING AND LOCATING

Athletes have always been watched closely to find out how they can perform better. Now, thanks to new technology, more and more athletes are having every breath and movement measured. Using this information, players and coaches can figure out how to improve performance. On the sea, people competing in sailing competitions turn to high tech to help them navigate better and avoid hazards.

Specialist GPS devices for outdoor sports work in even the worst weather and can pick up more signals than a smartphone.

EVERY MOVE YOU MAKE

Athletes now wear pieces of technology that record information about their performance. The Catapult OptimEye is as small as a wristwatch. It contains a powerful computer and can collect data on acceleration, direction, position, and the impact of a collision. More than 900 sports teams use this powerful piece of technology to collect data. The data is analyzed using special computer software.

Global Positioning System (GPS) tracking technology can measure distances run by an athlete, as well as route, time, and speed. This data gives coaches and players new insights into the action on the track or on the field. Spectators, too, can analyze every pass, kick, or run made by their favorite players or teams.

Another handy invention is radio frequency identification tags, or RFIDs. These tags can be placed on objects or clothing to provide information that is read by scanners. Football players in the NFL wear RFIDs to track their position and speed. This information is instantly transmitted to broadcasters, who share the extremely accurate statistics with fans.

MASTERING THE SEA

Sailors used to rely on paper maps, or charts, to figure out a route and keep on track. Now, this can be done on a laptop, tablet, or even a smartphone using GPS, online charts, and powerful software. Sailors can also be rescued more easily thanks to the latest Emergency Position Indicating Radio Beacons (EPIRBs). These small floating devices send rescue signals, which are picked up by satellites.

These black chest harnesses keep a Catapult OptimEye held firmly against an athlete's back. They can measure and analyze every movement.

VITAL SIGNS

New technologies in sport allow athletes to analyze many of their body functions. Athletes test themselves at rest and when active. They use electronic monitors to measure pulse, breathing rate, breath volume, blood pressure, and temperature. All this data is recorded using computer programs, such as BodyByte. These programs show athletes how to plan and manage their training and make performance gains. BodyByte also keeps track of an athlete's nutrition needs.

SPORTS MEDICINE

Athletes need to stay healthy. However, sometimes they can be injured. Sports medicine gets injured athletes back in the game as soon as possible. **Biomechanics** is part of sports medicine. It is a science used in sports to study how hits, tackles, speed, and other actions affect muscles and bones. Xsens is a Dutch company that makes 3-D motion tracking technology called MVN BIOMECH. This system uses tiny, tough tracking devices that can be worn by athletes. Data from the trackers travels wirelessly to a computer. A software program turns the data into 3-D animations that can then be studied.

Sports injuries often involve damage to delicate body tissues called **ligaments** and **cartilage** found in or around bones. Now, doctors can insert a thin fiber through a small cut in the skin to look at the damage. Then they can insert tiny tools to repair the damage.

Wearable devices mean that keeping track of your workout can be as easy as checking your phone!

TAKING IT TOO FAR?

Is it worth risking lasting injury, or even death, to win a game or a race? Sometimes medical technology is used for the wrong reasons. Some athletes take drugs to boost performance, even when sports officials have banned the drugs as too dangerous. In 2016, during the Rio Olympics, Russia was accused of allowing many of its athletes, from many different sports, to take drugs to improve their performance. As a result, many Russian athletes were banned from the Olympics. Do you think this was fair to the athletes?

TECHNO PLANET

Fitbit, Apple, TomTom, and Garmin all make wearable fitness devices as small as a necklace or watch. These exercise devices can track personal health. Some record a person's pulse and blood pressure, distances traveled, and calories burned during exercise. Data is stored online and can be downloaded to a computer or read on a smartphone app.

TECH TO THE RESCUE!

Sports are great for health and provide huge entertainment, but accidents will happen. That is when new technology can save the day.

MOUTH MAGIC

Modern mouth guards are more than a simple piece of plastic shaped to protect a player's teeth. One brand, FITGuard, alerts players to serious but invisible injuries, such as concussion. If a player takes a hard hit, the mouth guard lights up. These lights are bright enough for a coach or referee to see. Other brands are made of plastic that changes color when an athlete is overheating.

SPECTATOR SAFETY

Accidents do not only happen to athletes on the field. Sports stadiums draw big crowds of spectators. The safety of each one is important. There is a real science to moving crowds into, around, and out of stadiums quickly and safely. New stadiums have at least three wide **concourses**. These allow people to move more freely. There are different stairs, escalators, and elevators for spectators, staff, and service workers. Big entrance and lobby spaces make lines safer and security screening easier. All these safety features are made possible because stadiums can be designed and analyzed on computers using powerful software.

Sports facilities have always had first aid kits. Now they have **defibrillators** to help anyone having a heart attack. The newest models tell helpers how to attach monitor pads to a patient's chest and give a shock to a person's heart. These defibrillators can talk in English, French, and Spanish.

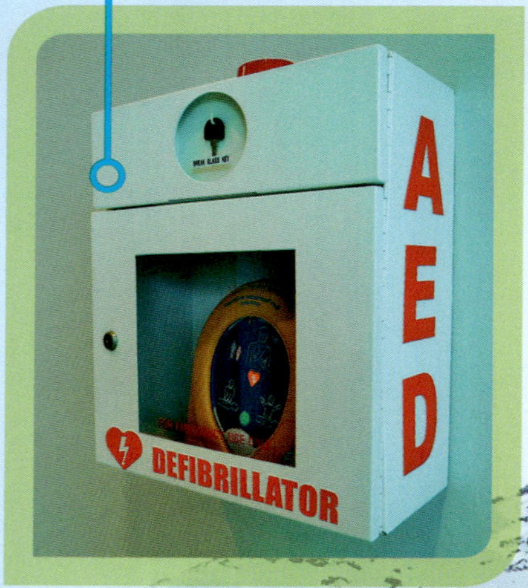

Most sports stadiums now have defibrillators. This piece of tech is easy to use and can save lives.

LOST AND FOUND

For wilderness and ocean sports, a personal locator beacon is a good way to call for help in an emergency. It signals satellites, not cell phone towers, and sends a precise GPS location. SPOT beacons can also send ordinary tracking signals to a phone or e-mails to say, "I'm at this location, and I'm OK!" To find lost hikers, skiers, and sailors, search-and-rescue technology uses a wide variety of tools. These include infrared and **thermal** imaging from drones and low-flying airplanes, and images from satellites.

The easiest way to search rough terrain quickly is by drones with cameras.

FITGuards are simple enough to fit in an athlete's mouth. To check the tech, just smile!

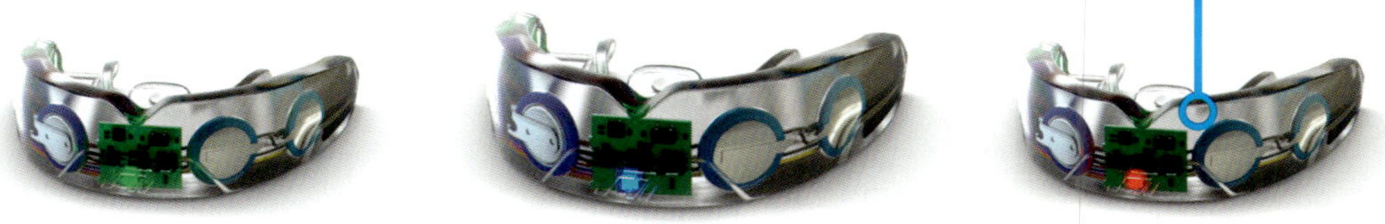

Green—low risk *Blue–moderate risk* *Red—high risk*

VIRTUAL SPORTS

New technologies mean fans can enjoy all the thrills and spills of the track, stadium, or great outdoors without having to leave home. Technology brings sports much closer to fans. Even if your favorite team is hundreds of miles away, you can still be there at the game.

JUST LIKE THE REAL THING

With a virtual reality headset and an app, you can feel as though you are right there at the stadium. The headset picks up video from 360-degree cameras, so you can look all around. The Spanish company First Vision makes on-player cameras and microphones. These feed video and sound to fans so they can see what the player is seeing. Fans can watch a player's health and performance statistics, too. First Vision's technology has already been used in hockey and basketball.

But what if you want to see the game from anywhere in the stadium? Dutch technology company Beyond Sports is working on this. It gathers data about players, officials, and fans, and turns that into a 3-D computer **simulation** of the game. You can watch this on a headset and experience the game from every angle.

E-sports events (see right) can be attended both online and in real life.

A NEW KIND OF SPORT

Video game technology has led to the invention of e-sports. These are sports played on computers. Professional game players have their own fans. These fans like to watch their heroes play, as well as play the game themselves. Around 160 million fans watch big games. By 2020, the number could reach 600 million. This is one sport in which physical fitness and skills are not factors—except for fast reactions!

Some virtual reality sports need special headgear for video or audio.

TECHNO PLANET

With virtual reality, it is now possible to recreate the social experience of a sports event. Stadiums and players can be shown in 3-D, and almost in real time. The fantasy sport app Ballr allows fans to engage online in real-time interactions during sports events. It does this using thousands of pieces of data from real games. Fans can use their smartphones and tablets to "step in" and view the game from anywhere and interact with other fans.

FUTURE FANTASTIC

In the future, there will still be professional athletes and their fans. There will still be people who enjoy playing sports for fun. New technology will continue to keep athletes healthier and safer. It will help coaches get the best from their teams. It will also find new ways for fans to interact with their favorite sports. However, no matter how sports technology changes, sports will still be about enjoying the game—win, lose, or draw.

BODY AND MIND

But, how do you know which sport is best for you? The answer could be in your **genes**. The Athletigen company in Nova Scotia is looking at ways to use the body's genetic make-up to figure out what our physical strengths and weaknesses are. This could help you choose the right sport and help athletes avoid injury and train more effectively.

Virtual reality sports experiences will become more **immersive**. Companies such as Google and Oculus are working on a new set of technologies called **telepresence**. Rather than creating an invented world when you put on a headset, telepresence will actually allow you to experience real places as though you are there. Robot cameras wirelessly linked to a headset will follow every head movement. Sports fans will not only enjoy the sights and sounds of a game, but also feel as though they are right at the game. Virtual reality is even being tested in space. Maybe, one day, games played on another planet will be watched from Earth.

ROBOT SPORTS

You need people to play sports, right? In some future sports, the only humans will be the spectators. Eventually, robots could be smart enough to kick a ball, hold a racket, or run a race. The Robocar is an electric race car that uses sensors and computers to drive. It takes part in a racing championship called Roborace. Can you imagine Formula 1 racing without drivers?

OVERCOMING DISABILITIES

Many future changes in sports will help athletes with disabilities. Wearable devices using sound and vibrations will guide athletes to make the right movements. New prosthetic limbs will be ventilated so athletes can wear them longer. The "Brainsled" is a headset idea that allows a bobsled rider to control the sled through brainwaves instead of muscle movements. **Electrodes** attached to the rider's head send signals to the sled's rudder, telling it which way to turn. These developments will allow athletes with disabilities to compete more equally with able-bodied athletes. Thanks to sports technology, the future of sport is looking bright!

Bobsled riders need strong bodies with fast reactions—but "Brainsled" riders can just use brainwaves.

No need for a driver's seat in the Robocar race car. It drives itself!

TECH TIMELINE

1776
Frenchman Jean-Moyes Pouzai patents the stopwatch

1890s
British company J. W. Foster and Sons develops some of the first running shoes with spikes

1920s
Adolf "Adi" Dassler (founder of the Adidas brand) makes the first modern running shoe

1935
Idea of virtual reality is first described—in Stanley G. Weinbaum's science fiction story "Pygmalion's Spectacles"

7th century B.C.E.
Ancient Greeks build gymnasiums as training grounds for sport and exercise

1872
Eadweard Muybridge photographs a running horse with a series of cameras

1916
Heuer markets the first sports stopwatch accurate to 1/100th of a second

1921
The first radio sports broadcast—a boxing match in Pittsburgh, Pennsylvania

1937
Tour de France bicycle race allows the use of the derailleur gear-changing system

1959 Canadian hockey player Jacques Plante invents the goalie mask

1974 Baseball player Tommy John receives the first ligament graft for repairing tendons in a pitcher's arm

1993 Hockey is the first sport to use goal-line technology

1996 HANS device introduced to support necks of race car drivers and reduce injuries

2008 Speedo LZR swimsuit introduced

1955 Hockey Night in Canada introduces "instant replay" to its television broadcasts

1962 Steve Russell, a student at the Massachusetts Institute of Technology (MIT), leads a team that creates Spacewar!, the first digital video game

1980s First graphite tennis rackets

1994 First use of helmet headsets for professional football quarterbacks

2001 Hawk-Eye technology used for the first time, at a cricket match between England and Pakistan

2016 Fantasy sport app Ballr is released

GLOSSARY

Please note: Some **bold-faced** words are defined where they appear in the book.

aerodynamics The properties of an object that affect how it passes through air, or how air flows around it

alloys Metals made from two different metals, or one metal and another material

amateur Someone who plays sport as a pastime, rather than as a profession

analysis Detailed examination

biomechanics The study of how different forces affect muscles and bones

compress To press so that an area reduces in size

concourses Open spaces in a stadium where crowds gather

concussion An injury to the brain caused by something hitting the head

data Information used to figure things out

defibrillators Devices that give an electric shock to a heart to make it beat again

electrodes Points where electricity flows into or out of something

electronic circuit A complete pathway that carries electricity

genes Parts of a cell that control how the body looks and grows

Global Positioning System (GPS) A navigation system that uses satellite signals to determine exact locations

graphene An extremely thin, but strong, material made from carbon

immersive Generating a three-dimensional image that appears to surround the viewer

impact The force of two or more things hitting each other

infrared Invisible light beyond the red end of the color spectrum

ions Atoms that have a positive or negative electrical charge

nutrition Food and nourishment

paralyzed When you cannot move part of your body

penalty A disadvantage imposed on a team for breaking a rule of the game

playback Watching videos of a moment in a sport to get new information

prosthetics Artificial replacements for a missing body part

sensor A device that can be placed in or on something to send information

simulation Something that is made to look or feel like something else

sponsor Someone who gives money to athletes to help them train and compete

telepresence Virtual reality technology that creates the sense of being somewhere else

thermal Caused by heat

three-dimensional (3-D) A shape having or seeming to have the three dimensions of length, width, and height

virtual reality An artificial, but realistic, experience of sights and sounds

LEARNING MORE

BOOKS

Editors of *TIME for Kids* magazine. *Amazing Sports and Science* (TIME for Kids Book of Why). TIME for Kids, 2014.

Gregory, Josh. *Sports Medicine: Science, Technology, Engineering*. Scholastic, 2016.

Johnson, Robin. *Paralympic Sports Events* (Winter Olympic Sports). Crabtree, 2009.

Swanson, Jennifer. *Super Gear: Nanotechnology and Sports Team Up*. Charlesbridge, 2016.

WEBSITES

http://findmespot.com
Learn how the SPOT tracker device works and how it can help those who play outdoor sports far from home.

www.csipacific.ca
See how the Canadian Sport Institute provides world-leading Olympic and Paralympic daily training environments for elite athletes and coaches.

www.exploratorium.edu/explore/sport-science
Explore the science of baseball, surfing, hockey, cycling, and more on the website of the Exploratorium in San Francisco, California.

www.sciencebuddies.org/science-fair-projects/Intro-Sports-Science.shtml
Find out how important science is in sport through projects and background information.

INDEX

About the Author

Paula Johanson is completing a Graduate Certificate in Digital Humanities at the University of Victoria, Canada. Her nonfiction credits include 34 books on science, health, and literature for educational publishers. Paula would like to dedicate this book to Erica and Johnny B.